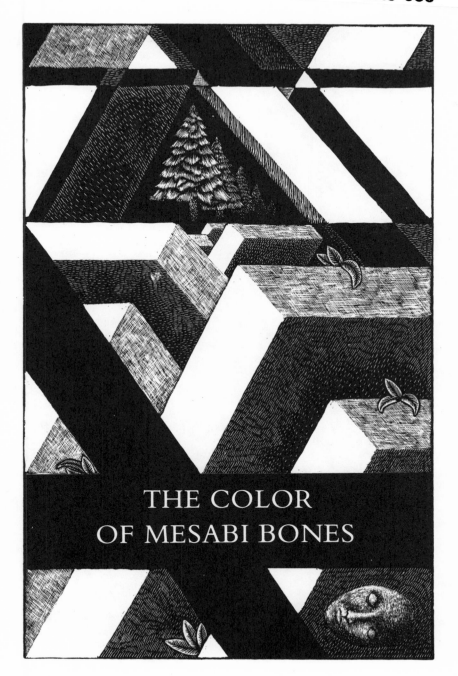

THE COLOR
OF MESABI BONES

The Color
of Mesabi Bones

Poems and Prose Poems

by John Caddy

Designed and Illustrated
by R. W. Scholes

M I L K W E E D   E D I T I O N S

THE COLOR OF MESABI BONES
© 1989. Text by John Caddy
© 1989. Design and Graphics by R. W. Scholes
All rights reserved.
Printed in the United States of America.
Published in 1989 by *MILKWEED EDITIONS*.
Post Office Box 3226
Minneapolis, Minnesota 55403

Books may be ordered from the above address.

92 91 90 89   4 3 2 1

Publication of this book is supported in part by grants from the Literature
Program of the National Endowment for the Arts, the Dayton Hudson Foun-
dation for Dayton's and Target Stores, the First Bank System Foundation, the
Jerome Foundation, the Minnesota State Arts Board with money appropriated
by the Minnesota State Legislature, with special funding from the McKnight
Foundation allocated through the Minnesota State Arts Board, the Arts De-
velopment Fund of United Arts, and by the contributions of many generous
individuals.

Library of Congress Cataloging-in-Publication Data

Caddy, John.
    The color of Mesabi bones : poems and prose poems / John Caddy
  : designed and illustrated by R. W. Scholes.
        p.   cm.
      ISBN 0-915943-40-9 : $8.95
      I. Title.
  PS3553.A313C6   1989   89-36393
  811'.54 — dc20   CIP

For Jerome Bach,

Teacher, Friend

Grateful acknowledgments to the editors of the publications in which the following poems first appeared: "The Quest in This Season," *Dakotah Territory*; "The Color of Mesabi Bones" and "Passage Rite" in *Great River Review*; "The Marriage of Salamanders," "Touching," and "A Party to Enormity" in *Milkweed Chronicle*. "A World War II Premium from Battle Creek" was first published, and "Passage Rite" reprinted, in *This Sporting Life*, Milkweed Editions (1987).

The author wishes to express gratitude to the Minnesota State Arts Board for a 1988 Artist Assistance Fellowship, and to The Loft for a 1987 Loft/McKnight Award, which made it possible for him to complete this book.

Special thanks to Rodger Kemp for his ear and his gentle persistence in helping with revision, to Sheila O'Connor, and to Cliff Carlson for the story behind "Mine Town: *Trick or Treat.*"

1 SOMETHING FOR EVERYONE

A Lozenge	13
Something for Everyone	14
The Giant	15
St. Austell, Cornwall	16
Mine Towns	17
Infinite Regression	19
Shaken Child	20
Forms Matter	21
A World War II Premium from Battle Creek	22
Mine Town: *Blasting*	23
The War Effort	24
Captain Tom	25
Submariners	26
Mine Town: *Edges*	27
The Faces of Ancestors	28

2 CHANGELING

The Changelings	31
The Dumb Kids	32
To Sing the Fire to Sleep	34
Home Movies	35
Yellowjackets	37
The Canterville Ghost	38
The Beating	40
Snow Forts	41
Who Said?	42
Mine Town: *What Are You Gonna Do?*	43
Mine Town: *Trick or Treat*	44
Abandonment	45
The Boy with Green Hair	46
The Tentative	47
Learning Ketchup	48

Touching 49
The Conspirators 50
Red Maples 51

3 THE MARRIAGE OF SALAMANDERS

Empaths 55
Scissor Man 56
Fluency 58
Sleep Tight 59
Circus and Transformation 61
Kiss Me Goodnight 62
The Falling of a God 63
The Travel Collection 65
The Marriage of Salamanders 67
Outward and Visible Signs 68
Passage Rite 69

4 FINDING THE SNAKE

Finding the Snake 73
The Man's Creed 75
Reading 76
Art Disguised 77
Extensions 78
The Mummy 79
Broken Arrow 81
The Tales of Hoffmann 82
Dreaming to Power 83
Mine Town: *Cultures Collide, A Quest Fails* 84
Acolyte 85

5 GYRFALCON

The Gyrfalcon 89
Terraria and Aquaria 91
As Long as Your Feet are Under My Table 92

Hibernation   93
Keeping Steady   95
The Invisible Boy   96
Surprise!   98
Mine Town: *Knowing Where You're At*   99
The Quest in This Season   100
School Maiden   101
The Length of These Generations   102
Mine Town: *Uncle Joe at the Ballgame*   103
A Party to Enormity   104

6 BRACKEN TIME

Bracken Time   109
Breakfast Meeting   110
Black Swan Dream   111
Permission   113
Mine Town: *Victory in Japan Day, Eveleth, MN, 1955* 114
Mine Town: *Being Screened*   115
Graduation Moment   116
Blanking Memory   117
The Elements So Mixed   118
A Love Triangle   119
All He Can Think Of   120
The Creature   121

7 THE COLOR OF MESABI BONES

The Color of Mesabi Bones   125

Index   131

*Something
for Everyone*

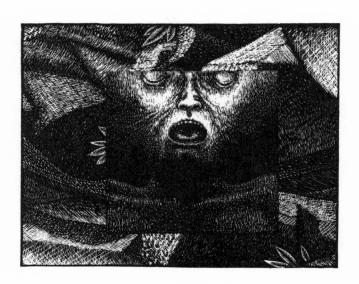

A LOZENGE

The child remains always
dangerous, alive but
blunted until a man's absent

tongue worries a key out
from some pocket
of memory and rolls it
over in the mouth, a lozenge of

whispers, of hair in firelight,
a mother's hand shifting
from cookstove to forehead, of
elephants straining to canvas,
locomotives' night steaming,

gypsy wagons, tricycle bells . . . rolls it
over until breath opens and eyes enlarge
and the child yawns,
waking — when the guilty start

stops it, the key
quickly swallowed, jaw
hardened, eyes again small, the man
resumed.

The woman never liked to be touched.
When she was a girl and her beau would park
the Model T and slip an arm around her shoulders,
she would lift it off and smile and say
You mustn't do that, you'll break my wings.

She would have preferred
parthenogenesis after two kids, but
she has to suffer the man, secretly
without diaphragm but with desire
for revenge and with desire
for someone of her own.

When the boy is born she hemorrhages
hours after delivery and almost dies before
the nurse slips in pooled blood.
The man is furious, knows he's been
abandoned for some thing.
She bleeds and bleeds, and during Unction
the priest tells her this is punishment
for marrying out of the Faith.

She names the boy a name which means
'Gift of love' and 'Gift of God.'
When the boy is three and four
and five, she tells him over and over how
when he was born she bled
and bled until she almost died.
Gift of love.

Grandpa and Grandma visit.
Over dinner something is said.
The man is the Giant again,
rants from the small-eyed face. The boy
watches, ready to run. The Giant
seizes the boy's eyes with his own:
You little devil, don't you
look at me that way! The boy
bolts from the table, the Giant
after him. The woman is yelling.
They run around the table,
through the living room. Grandpa
is yelling. The boy darts up the stairs
too tall for his legs. His brother
and sister stare silent. The Giant
catches him at the top of the stairs,
squeezes his sparrow arms and
shakes him, shakes — Grandpa
stops him with his hands. The man
is not that day allowed to hurt. Grandma
and stiff Grandpa put on their coats
to drive home. The man
stares at a wall. Grandma
keeps looking back as they go
out the door. The boy is two.

Great-grandfather Coad led blind ponies
up and down the dark tracks underground
from six years of age,

hauling the ore carts, patient hooves clumping
on ties, iron wheels rolling echoes up and down
the hollowed fossil sea.

For nine hundred days just before dawn he turned
his pale eyes to the sea, stepped into the cage
and fell down the shaft to his ponies.

The Cornish need sea, wet or turned rock,
mine drifts and beach dunes the saltsame smell.
Before that boy was done he'd carved holes
in the bones of three fossil oceans.

Orphaned at nine, he smuggled his minewhite
skin into the hold of a freighter America bound,
as his fathers dreamed of embarking
for the Summer Country or Avalon, dreaming
always West as they smuggled and mined.

He crept into the hold, trading dark for dark,
found a hollow in crates and listened to cargo
roll and thump in the waves of the living Atlantic,

boyman, a miner, missing the soft nuzzling
of his ponies whose lips would search out
the pasty scraps he'd save. His halfblind ponies.

A miner born, or made by nine, stowaway.
What could his children expect?
What would they grow?

Much abandoned now, forced out or grown over, gone,
thrown into memory's hole. You have to dig for it.
Water-filled pits, rusted washing plants and crushers.
Tracks and spurs that just stop. The white pine cut,
the iron dug out. Not even much red left. No dust
coating cars or ground into hands. But bones mix with ore
in these empty mines, and the bones are red.

Much has always died. Towns: old Mesaba, Adriatic, Elcor.
Old pavement weedsplit. Lost customs and recipes,
causes and countries. Words: *Poyka. Sisu.* Short old women
in black babushkas clumped in front of churches.
Sayings: *May the Devil carry you off in a sack!*
Whole languages: Serb, French, Italian, stubborn Finn,
merchants who could speak them.

Much has died. Some nourishes still. Strike dreams:
1907, the Wobblies in '16, the thirties, fifties — dreams
of a living wage, justice, victory. Lost homesteads and saunas,
Finnish dovetails still wedging the squared white pine.
Logging camps: a privy, a chimney half-standing.

Some refuses death: timewarp Friday nights
on Chestnut Street, bumper to cruising bumper, sidewalks
swirling, all the bars bright, everyone calling *Hey*
to everyone, the polka lilt to the voice and the eye.
Behind town, out in the woods in old jackpine slash,
polished cones grip their seeds like gray stones,
wait lifespans for the fire to bloom.

Much is buried for the digging. The Mill Forty:
tangled concrete roots of the world's largest sawmill.
Sprinkled through fields where the company

moved the houses off, open cellars choked with raspberries.
By the back steps, rhubarb still thrusts its spear,
comfrey sprawls, mints and lilies struggle with long grass.

Abandoned now, knocked down and forced out, thrown
into memory's hole, the shaft leading to the full heart
where it all and always is embraced and laugh–angry and alive.

The man is searching for himself.
Trying not to weep.
The mirror leaps with sons who wear his face,
who must be him but cannot be.
The mirror is a cheat, chafes
the dry streambeds of his cheeks.
It must be fogged. Wipes it roughly down
and tests his fear of seeing clearly once again.
The same. Hands upon the frame

jerks the mirror from the wall, shatters
it down on his louring skull
and wears sharp glass around his neck.
Mirror slices lie beneath his eyes,
which he would close now against the light,
but before his eyelids drop he sees
a smear of blood on every scattered face.
Abandoned now, he swears he'll teach these shards
to wear the face that names his fear.

The doctor slides the X-rays from manila,
clips them to the fluorescent wall
and I am seized in giant's hands and shaken into
two — *Look* — *these concretions here, the black*
lumps — bone burned into acetate —
notice the arm bones — *would appear*
that damage early — the giant squeezes
hard fingers around our bones, the child
holds — as a whipped dog presents its
throat — quiet, holds still to invoke
the rule of submission, hoping
rather awkward to say the doctor
murmurs *damage to the cervical vertebrae* . . .
the giant with small eyes shakes the child's
head a popping doll's head on a spring,
Calcareous knots on the bones, yes
this black but really white of course, a
negative — this is what the bones and meat
have always known — *We can't be*
optimistic, the injuries are old — *with*
patience perhaps? the arms the neck — the
buried child opening — *An X-ray syndrome*
. . . shaken child . . . we can't be sure
of course . . . I am sure. Finally. Wait
for all to stop so we can
breathe, wait to master stillness no
expression, hoping while the child
swells into now and fugues the giant's
always first words, *Don't give me that*
look! his sudden lunge, the chase — shaken
man, shaken child who never knew
the rules, or when the game began, or
even the number of players —
and I sit unmoving on the doctor's chair.

It is the timeless northern
white, the yearly time
to make things right. Bing
spins dreams at seventy-eight,
the woman and man have been up
late arranging toys under the tree.
The boy has just turned
three, his first Christmas
for meaning and memory.

He toddles last down the stairs
in his sleepers, not fast but one
careful foot at a time, awestruck
by this fiery tree and the toys
spread beneath. On the floor his
brother and sister already
scramble on hands and knees.
The boy's eyes are wide. He climbs
onto the couch next to the woman.

They all look at him surprised.
He stares at a yellow tractor
with a windup key and black
rubber treads. She feels his body tremble.
How are you? Outside still dark,
the tree — *Fine* — so fiery bright. *Why
aren't you playing with your toys?* Her
voice dreams of sleighbells and white.
He asks in wonder, *Toys are mine?*

A WORLD WAR II PREMIUM FROM BATTLE CREEK

Breakfast more than he could want,
he eats quickly every morning, takes seconds
to empty the Kellogg's cereal box
and knife out the enemy on the back.

Printed on PEP! box backs, three ways:
Hitler is black dots and brown
swung in a scowl, his mustache
a broken piece of pocket comb,
mouth slashed red dots in the brown.

Sides of riboflavin, thiamine,
but on the backs adrenaline:
Mussolini, mostly jaw, confetti dots of red
and two day whiskers sprinkled black
like Sunday comics magnified.

On each scowling Axis face,
concentric targets printed Red–White–Blue
so he can aim and score
the pocket knife or rock.

Tojo all dark yellow dots, except
for the buck-toothed white, and spidery
glasses outlined in black,

the boy's kindergarten favorite,
but Mr. Seigel at the Southside Store
hardly ever has Tojo in stock,
he's overstocked with Hitler.

A rock on the nose is a bullseye,
a hundred points. The boy prefers the eyes.
Tacked to the backyard tree, the cardboard skin
tears with a jagged rock but
will not bleed, and Tojo's glasses never break.

Arc lights, shadowlines
sharp as razor cuts.
Hardhats hunched into shoulders.
The fuse-spark leaps to the charge: *Fire
in the hole!* and the earth
breaks and sloughs part of itself,

the town shudders in the swelling
groan of rock and like
huge drunken footsteps
up the stairs, the house shakes
in the center of the night, plates
rattling in the hutch.
We kids would open eyes and think,
Blasting, and drop back.

It was a thing men did, and so,
awesome, admirable.
We thought no more of it—
but visiting relatives who'd gotten out,
who'd moved to California
to lose their memories in the sun,
would scream and run
into the halls in bedclothes.
And the plaster in the ceilings
spidered more every year.

After supper I'd use the can opener to cut the bottoms off the day's tin cans, slip the two end circles inside the open cylinder, place them on the linoleum, and — freedom of noisy freedoms — stamp them flat. What could he say? They were for the War Effort. We were all Patriots. We had Drives: paper, scrap metal, old tires.

We carried dimes in our mittens to grade school to slowly buy Bonds. The teachers sold us small red stamps with the Concord Minuteman on them, and we'd lick them into books. A full book meant — the teachers always said it in full — a United States War Bond. We figured a jeep, maybe even a tank's worth.

We learned to talk in Capitals. We had Drives and Victory Gardens, Blackouts and Spies. Victory Gardens, I knew, had to make a "V" shape in the earth or they wouldn't help the war.

Spies were all around. The mines were Targets. Once we saw a spy in a Piper Cub flying back and forth over the pits. He used a helio-graph only Scouts would notice, sun flashing off the plane's win-dows. We wrote each series of flashes down in Morse Code, but couldn't cipher it. We showed it to a soldier home on leave, but he couldn't break the code either.

Blackouts were best. Sirens would go off, house lights blink yellow to black window by window. From the front steps we watched night blot out the streetlights block by block until the whole town was unmade. We'd walk around the house with red cloth rubber-banded over flashlights. Air raid wardens appeared from the dark to inspect and complain about the guy up the block who didn't pull his shades. We'd sit in the living room and listen to the radio, kids dashing to the window now and then to peel back curtains and im-agine searchlights tunneling the sky, hoping for bombers, wonder-ing if this would be the time, until the All-Clear sounded. I learned something in Blackouts. I didn't know what, but I knew it was big-ger than our house. Think of it: a power so strong it could make parents sit in the dark.

CAPTAIN TOM

The Mine Captains were tough sons of bitches who arrived knowing what Jehovah knew. They wore Cornish names like Nichols and Pengilly, Cohoe and Quick, and they were always by God called Captain. Tom Caddy was Captain of the Hawkins Mine in this new world where the Cornish faces turned iron red.

The Captain was the bearing the mine spun on. He set pay by the foot and pay by the ton. He spoke flat to the miners, direct to the Superintendent, and up to no living man. Underground he talked *slicing* and *stopes, drifts* and *tonnage* and *timbering*, and at home he was silent or he proclaimed.

The Captain was called Tom only by his cronies. They liked to hunt. In Cornwall, the miners poached hares. On the new Mesabi, they hunted in buckskins and ate venison much of the year. *Bloody* this, *bloody* that, and *Jesus H. bloody Christ.* Once one of the dog pack groveled too much when blamed. Tom said, *Why can't the damned dog be a man about it?* None of them would ever swear in the presence of a woman.

Tom sought out a woman who agreed to be meek. He married at thirty, she at eighteen. She called him Captain, and ran him from that deference. Great-grandma Ellen was doilies and tea and a steely uncaring for all outside the blood. His father had married the same woman, his son would marry the same. After four or six or twelve children—do you count the dead?—in as many years, each of these helpless powerful women decided to sleep the rest of her life alone.

Most of the gas-ration stamps go for family obligation, so all of them pile into the Ford on Sundays, off to Grandma and Grandpa's. At the end of the trip, just before Nashwauk, there is a long curve where, rounding it, the school bell tower comes into sight in the distance, high above the straight-edge horizon of the mine dump. When they see it, the man and kids play war movie, cry *Submarine!* and *Up periscope!* and become the Ford's crew, crying *Fire one! Fire two!* After firing, they chant seconds out loud, and the kids make explosions in their throats when the torpedoes reach the tower.

The Ford is rocked by depth charges, the man lurching the car back and forth with the wheel to evade them. As they drive closer, the bell tower slowly, elegantly as a doomed passenger liner, sinks toward the surface, and they watch batebreath as the tip of the bow finally slips below the horizon, and cheer. Just as the Ford dives under the railroad bridge and plunges into the sea that took the tower, they are in town. They are all below the surface now, suddenly quiet, tubes empty, hoping against depth charges.

After the afternoon and the women's faltering visit talk, kids trying to stay busy and out of the way, and everyone pretending it is air they are in and not this family-thick amnion, after repeated bubbles of *Fifteen two!* and *Go, Godammit!* exploding above the cribbage board where the red-faced officers contest, they all drive off into the dark. When they pass under the bridge, they do not drop ballast to rise dripping but safe again into moonlight, but stay submerged on the seafloor, hull breached, the crew separately encased in whatever breathing apparatus each can invent, periscopes down, silent running for home.

Always on the edge. Open pits ring the town,
dumps and stockpiles ring the pits
carved down in wide red terraces where
fifty foot draglines small in the depths
scoop up blasted rock. Ore trains and trucks
work their way up the long spirals.
On the horizon, galvanized crushers
and washing plants, conveyor belts.
Company houses teeter close to the brink.
The pits mouth vast open vowels at the town,
the edges pocked with empty foundations.

Mine town voices, always on edge. From the bars
lining main street—the Magic, the Royal, Niv's,
the Crystal—words pelt the sidewalk like hail
or tumble out warm rain, words brinked
on anger and pitched to laugh back, same time.
Always loud—the Corner, Elks, Ormond, Moose,
Arrowhead, the Legion, Klink's—a lot of men's talk
edges blood, circles salt without knowing.
The women laugh too soon, know that, and laugh.

The boy dreams again he runs through
the lightless drifts and galleries of an underground
mine, face and shoulders tensed against repeated
blows he cannot prepare for. Ahead and behind,
his grandfathers and great-grandfathers wait
to ambush him. When light blazes, the cut rock
turns mirror and fills with faces. He runs.

These old Cornishmen, underground for life,
whose faces learned to be the fractured
rock they spent their bodies to break, iron against
raw stone, this bore and blast and shovel
which turned faces bleak as the winter
Atlantic breaking the Cornwall coast.

In the mines there were no faces of wives
who would not forgive this ambush
of their sons, no faces of the scared boy
except the one held inside, the one
forced to watch his sons and sons' sons
driven inside, generation after generation,
the light of each face snuffed as the child
is gagged and thrust into the hole.

Family and the narrow rowhouse
was a place to leave, to step in the cage
and drop into the drifts, to slog down
tunnels of night in a clump of hard pale faces,
the dark pressing in on the head's candle,
to mine, to beat on rock and hope the muscle
would wear enough that a man could go
safely home, that his face could mirror stone,
the rock absorb enough of his gall.

2

Changeling

He huddles in the pantry at Grandma's,
finger tracing the embossed mermaid
on the leather cover, eyes locked
in Hans Christian's tale. He reads
to leave the linoleum where once
he was content with clothespins.

He knows if he is any more here
today with these people who claim
blood relations—who will not confess
they stole him—the cold will grow
and the man will stop the car
to cut a switch tonight.

So for this time, he enters the mermaid.
He finds her love confusing, her strange
wish to leave the sea and walk
on stumping legs. To be away, apart,
to flow the green sea and watch
the human from distance, this he grasps,
but her wish, her love, slips through him.

But when it is time for her cruel proof,
his feet curl to the knives in her raw soles
and his legs draw up in her white agony.
He is amazed that some other knows, has
known, this pretending to human,
changelings together from an element
other than this, fishes gulping fire,
unable to scream, unable to return.

Recess. Kidswarm, nearly all bigger than Kenny and the boy. Fifth graders being airplanes, cursing and strafing these first graders when they get in the way. Swings and shoves and pom-pom-pullaway. But a part of the swarm has moved off the sand, over to the grass on the side of the building. He and Kenny run to look, thinking *fight*. He sees Dumb Billy in the center, and is afraid.

He doesn't know Billy, just knows he's one of the Dumb Kids no one talks about. But huge lanky Billy is in the center of something, and his malformed voice is shouting. He bends down, and the little kids wriggle closer to see.

Billy has Nancy down on the grass, shouts and grunts at her. She is crying, he has pulled her dress up. Chubby Nancy is womansized but minded as a child. The kidswarm watches Billy flip her over on her stomach and pull her panties to her ankles, the flash of darkness. He holds her down with his knee as he spanks her, his long awkward hands flailing down, slap and grunt and sob the only sounds. Everyone watches, more arriving all the time, but no teachers.

The boy is afraid. He senses that others are, too, but fascinated more. No one will help Nancy in her howling. For the first time he is in the center of a creature he instantly half-knows, a creature tense and leaning forward. Something inside each of them has leaped out of their bodies and connected them tendon to bone.

He feels the creature stirring in himself, grabs Kenny and runs with him to the door, struggles it open, runs to find the principal. When they burst into her office, all the boy can say is *Dumb Billy is spanking Nancy and he has her pants down and you better hurry*. He wants to say there is something wrong with everybody out there, but he can't. The principal says hard-lipped that those children can't help the way they are, and you shouldn't refer to them that way, and she is out of the office before the boy has understood that she meant the Dumb Kids.

There was something about it. He feared it, but something about it spoke to him of power, woke a new voice inside him that he wished were dumb. He feared it would shout and grunt like Billy.

The boy is in the fire. He is trying
not to cry. Flakes of ash dance out
his mouth while through the smoke
of roots he sings of how
behind his eyes the tears burst
into steam and score into his flesh
the face he learns to wear to let him
sing inside the flames. He will not blur
this pain with tears, tries to
sing the fire to sleep, but no one
hears the song as sung, for his corded
throat is prelude to a scream.
He is the singer in the fire, who has
determined not to cry, who wears the face
which holds his song within the flame,
but costs the blessing of tears.

As the camera pans, the people at the lawn party mug and work ex-aggerated words with silent mouths. They are all grownups in Kenny's black and white summer backyard, all dressed-up and drinking. Kenny and the boy watch a home movie in the basement. There is no sound. Kenny's mother is in the center of the screen now. She looks like laughter as she drains her glass and throws it over her shoulder. She puts her knees together and smooths her party dress all up and down with her hands, smiling at the camera, tossing her hair. Black lipstick and a white face. She reaches down to her hem and begins to lift. The picture wobbles on the screen. She slowly raises her dress to the tops of her stockings, lets go. The people in back clap silently, Kenny and the boy intent in the dark. The picture jerks. She reaches way up under her dress with both hands, doing something the boy can't figure. Making faces like an actress, she slowly pulls her panties down under her dress, steps out of them—one foot, stumbles, other foot—waves them gaily over her head. The other men and women clap and wide their mouths and show teeth. The screen goes white. While it rewinds the boy asks Kenny why she took off her pants. Kenny doesn't know. The boy wonders why Kenny showed him, but he doesn't ask. He wants to see it again.

The next day they sneak down the basement of Kenny's dad's department store to look at naked dummies. The boy is anxious, going down the back stairs, ready for the opened mystery. But when he sees the dummy breasts, they are just round things with no red in the middle. When Kenny slowly lifts one dummy's dress up, announcing like a circus man, the hidden part is just a blank smooth nothing. The boy gets mad. At first Kenny laughs, but he gets mad too, and throws open a storeroom door. The room is filled with a tumble of pink body parts, legs and arms, heads and middles all confused, men's parts and women's parts tangled, nothing between their legs, faces smiling dazed.

When the boy imagines first love years after, the dummies return in dream. The willing girl he undresses owns only the smooth blank. When the boy sees it, he jumps up the department store stairs and out the alley door into the silent lawn party, people miming words and showing teeth. The woman begins to lift her dress. The boy knows she will be blank there, is frantic to shut the projector off.

Wearing eyes of light as only
brand new creatures wear, Buck
clumsies through brush back of the cabin,
picking up burrs in his thick puppy fur,
and bumbles into a yellowjacket nest
in jackpine slash. They whirl into him,
burrow through fur to his skin and whine
his nose yellow as he howls blind—the boy
frantic with the pup's pain, beating them off.

The boy stands in the lake, holding
Buck's nose above water, trying to drown
the hornets, not feeling his own stings.
He digs fingers through fur for the buried ones
as they sting over and over, pulls them out
one by one and crushes them.

Wrapped in a towel, the pup shivers
in spasms from the poison, eyes
dull and staring, the boy unable to help
and unable not to feel. Shivering,
he connects with the woman's stunned look,
her incomprehension. He wonders
what her eyes were like before.

The boy sweats awake, dreamed wet again
by *The Canterville Ghost*, those first scenes
where the Black Knight charges terribly
with his lance leveled, and Charles Laughton
turns coward and quails, whips his horse
to his father's manor and hides in a pantry
off the kitchen, where he tries to not
breathe as the searchers arrive, the noble
men who would see honor done, listens again
as his stony father denies both knowledge
and possibility of his son's act. *Surely, then,*
the men say, *the lord could have no objection*
to our walling up the pantry?
The listener's panic catches *It would*
in his breath *settle matters, would it not?*
And satisfy honor. And again it's the dreamer
who will be buried alive, who watches
with horror but not surprise as the last brick
is mortared, who keeps silence until
the brick approaches the hole, the dreamer who
breaks, screams *Father!* and wakes wet as
the brick is set in, while the man refuses, for honor,
to hear, continues fictions with his guests
as the mortar and the boy's throat dry.

He doesn't dream the rest: the ghost of the son,
doomed to haunt manor and descendants until
redeemed by Margaret O'Brien and billeted G.I.'s.
The father has kept the code. Terror
makes the dream, not betrayals. The boy
can anguish those, but never feel surprise.

He falls back into the closed-loop movie
dream, the word *Father* a way of making
ghosts, transparent sons begging to be heard,
fathers unable, for honor, to hear.

The boy is dreaming in the dark
a metronomic sound that punctuates
the night with glares of sullen red.
It is, slow and strong, the sound
of one hand slapping
some boundary of meat.

Above this rise two muffled voices
intertwined like bindweed on the corn.
Their words are slurred and full of teeth.
The dark voice chants of heat and rage,
the woman's winds around it
a bewildered sodden begging.

The boy starts up, and stares,
and calms himself. In the dark
gets up and shuts the open closet door.

The boy has seen abandoned
Antarctic camps in *Geographic*
photos made years later by other
expeditions. Thick ice coats
everything, here a wall collapsed
from the growing pressure,
a chair overturned, there
a preserved table setting, unmoved
cup on the saucer. Even
the lightbulbs are rimed with ice.

The man has not spoken for days.
When his hand turns the doorknob
the long night begins again.
At table no one more than glances
from the plate. He makes
no requests, sits on the couch, drinks
whiskey on the rocks, expects to be
served, his cold pressure a glacier
obliterating all in expert slow motion.

The boy crawls through the tunnel
of his snow fort to the alabaster
chamber at the end, the round secret
place, and sits enclosed in walls
of white cold, winter light sifting through
the roof, sits safe, practicing white.

WHO SAID?

The stranger on the trike is half his age.
Without decision he is at her.
What are you doing here? Demands
she speak: *Huh? Huh? Answer me!*
Bullies her until she bawls. *Who said*
you could be here? Who said? Trembles

in shock: the man's *way* spewed from
his own throat. It's the dreamsplit again,
his eyes hang in air watching
the blind marrow below tear at the girl
who shrivels on her trike, waits

for what will come. He watches
himself run down the alley. How did
the man's voice get inside him? Who said
what he said? He avoids little kids for years.

Range women know to laugh.
Laughs hardcandy brittle
or easyround as coffee mugs.

They laugh before they're done
when they speak of themselves,
laugh to complete their sentences.

They know they laugh too soon, say
What are you gonna do?
and laugh all the unspoken words.

One of the little Carlson boys plays at his Grandma's and bored, rummages in her dresser, which he is not to do. Finds funny white robes packed with sachets in the bottom of one drawer, pulls them out. There are two, huge with separate pointy heads, big eyeholes sewn with tiny neat stitches. Sorcerer's robes, costumes for grownups, magic—imagines them at the Halloween party. Exciting new pictures of Grandpa and Gram.

He puts a head on. It blinds him until he adjusts the eyes. They'd have to take them off to bob for apples. The hoods would be perfect, though, for pin the tail. When Grandma surprises him like that she says *Jesus!* and yells, swats him on the bottom and says to never go in her drawers again! He looks later—the robes are gone.

When he thinks of it next he is thirty, says *Jesus Christ!* and can't quite imagine Grandma and Grandpa at the party.

ABANDONMENT

A mouth opens inside his chest
and forms a word without sound
but hard and wishboned and bright—

this is the face that harries the men
down the generations

while the secret mouth drives it from below
into the throat which trembles with the need
and must stay mute, so

the cheek hot, the taut lip
which dare not spill its silence.

Throat shoves it north into the face
whose mask contorts with the fishboned word,
whose eyes wear the bright soundless word—

this is the face the man wears,
this is the face the boy wears

in the ambush of tears that cannot be born.
They twist and press the bone back
against this pressure, this wanting

face the others misname, the mask
they name rage but cannot see through

to the wild grieving mouth that dreams
inside and wakes to speak but can't.
What is the word that cannot be said?

Hide or they get you. Everyone has to hide. Everyone he knows does, or tries. Some kids can't. He sees a strange movie, part Technicolor and part black and white. The color part is Dean Stockwell waking up one morning with his hair turned bright green. The black and white is horror: newsreel pictures of DP camps or concentration camps, hordes of hands on thin wrists stretching out through barbed wire.

The boy can't figure out why the kid's hair turned green. But he thinks of the confirmation stuff— *the outward and visible sign of an inward invisible*—what? It doesn't matter. Keep the inside inside. He likes the green hair, but agrees when the kid pulls a stocking cap over it.

The people who see the movie are supposed to be shocked when the kid who wakes up green is tormented for it by others. The boy is not. He already knows that stuff. What startles him is the switch from black to color to black. Just like real. Outside and inside. And the strength of those thin wrists. He doesn't think movies should be like that.

The man is speaking to the boy,
who is wanting, who is wary.
His voice reminds the boy
of another time this happened,
when the voice was dark and warm

as the lake that summer night
they looked into the water
from the end of the dock.
They talked.
Their bloods fluttered

like the fringed lips of clams until
the taste in their mouths of
other who was self
and panic slammed them shut.
When he blurred his eyes
the netted stars were caught.
Nothing came of it.

He looks up at the man, lip
hardens on one, then both.
They withdraw once more
into their solitary skins.

Dinnertime, digestion dependent on the man's
forbearance, the woman ready to be accepted
or be flayed, children wan and seated,
the formal requirements of Table.

The boy sits nearest the man, in his reach.

Tonight, meatloaf and potatoes, creamed
corn, homemade bread, lettuce, dills,
the ketchup bottle, tall and narrow-necked.

Table is the place for all to learn eating
from the man, who never grasps how
they can be so blind to his correction.

!—The boy hammers the end of the bottle again, no
ketchup, !— hammers, no ketch—the man abruptly
snatches it away, shows him How, rapping
the bottle neck against the edge of his hand.
It doesn't work. Doesn't work. Doesn't! The man
lifts the stubborn open end to his eye, stares it

down while a quirky deathwish in the boy's arm
bypasses his brain and calmly reaches across plates and
openhanded almost nonchalantly pops the bottle bottom.

Table frozen, forks halfway to mouths—a sudden red
gluts the man's right eye. The boy will die. Knows it,
can't believe—but cannot hold his laugh, the woman
squeezes her mouth but explodes, brother, sister
all rocking, rocking, and finally the redeyed man himself
cannot but laugh and laugh, the boy unbelievably alive,

the man for once himself the fool, for once seeing red and laughing.

The clothesline hums with fear.
The boy watches from the corner of the house.
The man is going to beat the dog,
ears flat and withers shrinking,
who can never believe this is happening.
All of them are living in their throats.
The man is red, the boy is pale,
both are trying not to cry.

The boy is caught within another laying on of hands,
at the cabin when they cleared the brush
and the wheelbarrow piled with branches
was too much for him, when the birch turned switch
and laid open his skin.

The dog presents his throat and yelps again.
He grips his forearm where
the scars lie white across the tan.

With a gun. A knife. With a car.
Tip the canoe. Bury him alive—
Up to the neck and cut out his tongue!
In whispers they dare from bed to bed
as the shouts and slaps rain on,
whispers in darkness, considering ways.
They are matter-of-fact, but the boy
is astonished and warmed
that big brother would share
such a private unspeakable dream.
Cut off his eyelids, stake him out.
In the sun! Tie him tight.
They have never been closer.
Pour boiling lead in his ear.
It is night's center, the fantasy root,
each method cupped long in the mind
and offered in whispers,
each rasp of the throat
more grotesque and headier wine.
Lure him to quicksand—
Like the Mummy!
and watch as his fist disappears.
Do it together with hatchets.
Throw him off the edge of the pit.
They plot on in the dark in whispers—
Just get him so mad he burns up!
—that break into giggles. They have never
been closer, such brothers, so warm,
while downstairs the blows rain on.

It is just that he wants to give the woman
some autumn leaves for the mantlepiece,
for the fall of things, as the family leaves
the cabin to head back to weekday town,

and it's his search for the perfect
that has led him so far, always
just over there a patch of brighter maples,
a more excellent shape,

and when he does find them—reds to weep for
in perfect sprays—his jackknife
slips in their cutting and slashes.
In the blink before the wound bleeds
he sees into his wrist—meat, yellowfat, cut
veins, then the red welling

panics, flings the knife, keeps the leaves
unknowing, bashes through the dapplesun
woods unsure of the road, yellow
aspen swirling to his knees until
the Ford brakes and everyone mad
and his hand red as the leaves it holds,
the other squeezing the cut wrist.

So he stands on the green between
gravel ruts in front of the car
watching the man yell through the windshield
about where the hell he's been, what the hell's
wrong with him, blood spotting the leaves
as he stands to his dressing down.

He says nothing but walks to the woman's
window, holds out the maples
in his glued wrists and her afraid to
take them, rolling down the glass
then *O God he's bleeding*

and the boy slowly aware that the sprays are
more and more wet with blood
stands there trying to give the ruined leaves
to the woman, for the falling of things.

3

The Marriage
of Salamanders

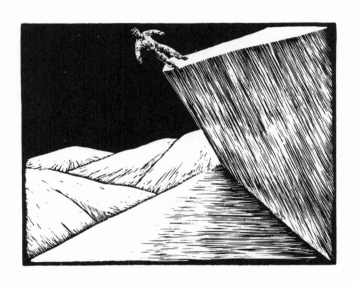

Each male here wants life to be
a silent Arctic waste, one
black heroic dot trudging into
endless white — but

the boy knows what the man
feels, he cannot

help being
inside the man who
cannot help being
inside the boy,
knows what
the son feels, in these
abandoned moments

all boundaries dissolve,
skins melt — each
desperate for the Arctic,
the black singular dot
forever trudging —

but fusing as if napalmed
into this Siamese violation,
this hot joined

outrage of not knowing
where he ends,
this terror of admitting
where he begins.

Three darks of him gleamed when they caught light:
the handsmooth oak of his grinding wheel frame,
an eye from deep under his hat, the old bronze of his bell.
We followed him. He was mystery, the stranger from outside.

Once every Spring we heard his handbell far away,
and blocks down the sidewalk under the elms
he would appear, a bent squiggle of dark.
Kids would holler *Scissor Man*, gather in clumps
to watch him trudge closer under his load.

He never spoke to kids, never looked.
He wore all black under his widebrimmed leather hat,
a leather pad between his packframe and bent back.
A sandstone wheel in a tripod of wood rode him high,
swayed with ditty bags lumpy with hints.

He never tried to get kids to like him.
I liked him for that. Once a year we heard him cry
Scissor Man, Scissor Man, knives and scissors, Scissor Man
and lift his arm and ring the bell again.

He touched his hat to housewives as he set up his rig,
the folding seat and the foot-treadle drive.
While he ground knives by someone's back door, we'd
make a scuffing cluster on the sidewalk, watching. When
he was done we followed him. It had always been this way.

Once a kid ran out in front of him to jeer, dancing back —
the Scissor Man stopped and studied him.
The kid's mouth closed, his feet froze. Those eyes
gleamed out at him from under the hat, but the Scissor Man's
mouth didn't move. Then his left hand sketched a sign,
and the kid ran home silent and wouldn't answer. That was
lore.

We'd walk till we were too far from home, and watch him
shrink down the sidewalk under the elms, the bell
lasting longer than the eye. He never did talk.
Never heard him say a word beyond *Scissor Man, Scissor Man,
knives and scissors, Scissor Man.* He was *outside,*
the stranger in black. He gleamed. Sharpened. I followed him.

Miss Prusha's oak yardstick would suddenly thwack! my left hand across three rows of desks. Our penmanship teacher hated the left and loved the right and true, which was named The Palmer Method. So she made me curl my left hand above the line I wrote on, and slant the endless exercise lines and ovals to the right, so I could at least approximate beauty. I did not.

In second grade she told me what "left" meant in Latin and French, and claimed that some countries exposed their left-handed children to the winter.

Refusing to be right, I curled my wrist and dipped cheap nibs into inkwells, my stubborn hand smearing each line as I wrote down the page. All through grade school, clouded blue papers, the words blearing in darker blue, a blue tattoo on my left hand's heel that I hid in my pocket like a brand that said *sinister* and *gauche*.

For a time, I wasn't left-handed. Except for writing and eating, I decided, I was ambidextrous: I could switch-hit in baseball and hockey, I could throw right-handed. Not well, but dextrously.

Toward the end of grade school, I found redemption and ended my shame. A passage rite of northern boys happens at night near a streetlight after a fresh snow, when the snowbanks and lawns beckon to be adorned. It was less a contest than a group celebration. We each staked out a pristine patch of white, exposed ourselves to winter and peed our names into it. My first efforts were jeered. But I was ambidextrous, I told myself, and was inspired to use both hands. Oh, my name was suddenly lovely, sweeping Palmer Method loops and curves and lovely round Os, peed two-handed into snow. Fluency at last!

My Method became the style that winter on the Southside. No beckoning snow was safe from our night fluencies. And no boy among us admitted there wasn't quite enough room for two hands.

The boy is climbing into bed.
Preparations are complete:
bedspread folded cleanly at the foot,
topsheet knifed across the blanket
he can almost ring a quarter on,
the smooth ellipse of pillow at the head.
Standing on the bed he
leans and snaps the lightswitch down,
lifts the covers from the center
and slides feetfirst into the taut cocoon he's spun.
He tightens the bedclothes under his chin
and puts away his hands. Every bedtime now
he summons up this cloth geometry.
He fears that in the waking, all will be undone.

The room is restless, shadow washed.
Scraps of headlights float the walls
and sweep across the ceiling crazily.
The boy wants to be the pure
yellow line at the bottom of the door.
He finds his heartbeat in his ear.
A carhorn blares his neck to goosebumps,
each standing hair polishes
what is hidden in the dark.
He cannot hold. Awash with shreds of night
the bed lurches from the floor, fingers
grip the edges of the mattress
and boy lies rigid as the bed lifts and tosses
toward a distant shout.

He will not enter this flight:
Pushes thumbs against squeezed eyelids,
burns patterns on his retinas to summon back

the ritual, quiets the flight
and rides it to the maple floor.
Breathes in. Ignores the barking dog. Breathes in.
Arms to sides again, the boy
aligns himself against the choreography of night.

CIRCUS AND TRANSFORMATION

The grasses drying to brown sway in the empty field
on Sauntry Hill north of the pit, grasshoppers keening
with the sense of *almost* we name August.

But overnight trucks and bright wagons appear, tiger roars,
sweet aromas of horse and straw and elephant, shouts
and coffee pails, lion coughs, a dishpan banged with a spoon.
Boys arrive on bikes all morning to work for free passes,
stretch the bigtop canvas with the men, a hundred of us
crouched and stumbling backwards, pulling the compass round.
We watch four foot tentstakes sink smooth into ground inside
a ring of roustabouts driving mallets in a whirl of muffled thuds.
Harnessed elephants slowly hoist the tentpoles as handlers
cajole them, teams of horses thunder by in shouts of
Make a hole there! and August becomes all possibility.

We crane our necks, see everything: cooktent, performers,
instant clotheslines full of wash, midgets, cages, sideshow tents,
maybe Clyde Beatty himself in trademark boots and jodhpurs.

That night, the bigtop: whipcracks and hoops of fire,
three-ring tightrope and spangles and big cats.
After the show, we sneak under canvas into the only place
we have no pass for, the back end of the freakshow.
We watch a lady with a little pot and big tits dance naked,
and after that she does something with a pony
on a wooden framework before they notice us and chase us out.
We are mightily confused, walking past the spotlit tiger cages,
and the only clear feeling is sorrow for the pony, the way he's tied.
But while we search for bikes in trampled grass and swear loud,
the unclear feelings circle large and sharp, a humming
behind them of *almost* that is like waiting, but in reverse.

In the dark he rubs raw
fingernails on new sheets like
chalk scraping slate until
she opens the door to

yellow hall light. Arms
braced on the bed, she
pushes her pursed lips close
for a dry kiss. The goodnight
is owed, her insistence
matter-of-course as his
recoil, but the kiss

more than kiss: hunger
that blots him out like ink
spilled in a starred sky,
a dark thing that stands
in the cavemouth and sends
him scrabbling deeper inside.

He suffers her, shrunken,
scrapes nails on sheets when
she closes the door. And she keeps
coming back, never surprised.

He'd yelled back at our father,
so he was that night forbidden doors,
and unwilling yet to knock the old man down.
Just a high school kid, but to my child self
he was Apollo, my older brother, God.
For him I swiped the basement clothesline,
snuck it in my shirt, tied it to
the radiator in the upper room we shared.
Past the dark first floor windows
he shinnied down into the tulips
and fled his shadows down the street.

I was afraid to crack the bedroom door for hours.
When our father made his heavy steps upstairs
I hugged myself in holy fear — Bill was gone
and I was very there — but the habit of silence held.

Three handfuls of earth thrown wild
rattled off the siding until he
found his aim and hit the window hard.
The light was out but I hadn't dared to sleep
and spent the night ticking with the clock.
But he was God. I lowered the rope
to his drunken weaving in the ruins of flowers.

It was clothesline, too thin for hands,
and he was clumsy with the drink.
Halfway up, trying to keep his feet from glass,
and up — and down he slid on ropeburned hands.
Again, again. The burning blossomed into blood.
And from below his drunken voice, *I can't . . . I can't.*

He started up again. I braced myself and leaned
and pulled, together we grunted up until
his elbows gripped the windowsill. Then
he almost fell, and clung to my skinny embrace
as I drowned in his whiskey breath.
We got him in. Our father did not wake.
To my small self this mad climb was the falling of a god.
I shrank from him. Would not smile.

Some days the boy receives twenty-five thick envelopes. In his room the collection spills off shelves. Every piece pored over, classified. He covets a wire display rack that spins. The pictures are good. Words are best. New Mexico, Land of Enchantment. Kachinas. Pueblos. Color. Space. Florida orange groves. Magic tourist countries: Cuba, Jamaica. Trinidad. The Carribean. Lesser Antilles. Windwards. White sands, ocean blues, pale to azure to green. Colorado mountains. The Cascades. Space and air. Popocatepetl. Hawaiian birds. High Sierras. Glacier.

Early on, the mailman is cheerful. After a few weeks of free pamphlets from every state tourism office and several small countries which advertise in the *Geographic*, in the back where the military schools are, he scowls up the walk, and the dog is uneasy at this change.

His worlds widen when he discovers *Holiday* magazine at the barbershop: Tahiti. Australia. Singapore. He filches coupons like a pro, sharpening his knife to an X-Acto point, dextrously drawing it down the edge of a dotted line while hiding it all under his hand. Got Rio. Got Canary Islands. The trick, in the barbershop waiting chairs, is to change the knife's direction without turning the magazine sideways. The trick is to grow hair fast.

When he comes home from school in early dark, he slips up to his room and gets out Samoa, Cuba, anywhere with sand and sun. After supper and fighting dishes with his sister, back up the stairs to climb mountains, raft rivers, check rates. Or another mailing binge: envelopes, coupons, Dear Sirs.

He never talks about the travel collection to anyone. Certainly not to his friends. He tries to catch the mail before his parents do. They shake their heads when it crosses their eyes. Pressed, he only says it's interesting. He lines them up by region—Pacific, US, Carribean—reads them for hours.

One Saturday, collecting on his paper route, he is asked by a woman if he has any hobbies. Disarmed, made bold by a stranger, he admits to a travel collection. The woman turns and yells, *Harry, the paperboy collects the same thing you do!* A man in longjohns and overalls grins to the door and insists on showing his collection. The boy is surprised to have company, uneasy. Foreign food smells. The couple live on the second story of a house near the foundry and the pit. The man grins behind the hand that hides his missing teeth. He reads folder headlines to the boy, sounding out the hard words: *Barbados. Montana. Antigua. Tehuantepec. Kachinas. Land of Enchantment.*

He is not to move.
The old fraternity paddle cracks
on his skinned-down buttocks again and again.
The boy has come to know
he can welcome this burning.
It is his familiar, which has grown
into a power.
He will not cry out, not weep, will not react.
Heat can be hoarded and used.
The man's arm trembles in what he thinks of as
restraint, and cracks down again.
The boy's eyes are on the aquarium between the beds
where two spotted newts struggle
to mate, the male's arms
locked around the female's neck, his belly
stretched along her back, his hind legs squeezed
around her bulging abdomen.
She is larger, but
twist and convulse as she may, she cannot dislodge him.
They thrash together
in the green weeds and ooze, then sink
slowly, until another lashing of her tail
shoves them toward the surface again.
She is trying to get to air.
A wide bubble forms as she arches her neck and opens
her mouth, and the male tightens his grip.
The bubble escapes. They sink.
The boy cannot look away.
He is not to move.
It would break all rules.

You're the spitting
image of your father!
The woman says it to
make emptiness between them.
Great-aunts in black say it
with a malice thrill.
Bluff men say it as
they swallow his hand.
He cannot stand this talk.
He has heard it for years.

In confirmation class he learns of
'outward and visible signs'
of inward invisible
graces and corruptions.

When he stares
into the bathroom mirror
he cannot see it.
When he looks
into himself at night, in bed,
he chokes on it.

In church he is beginning
to sense the power of repeated words.
And he wonders where
in that expression
does the spitting fit?

They call them Wet and Dry,
two abandoned pits concealed in woods and hills
south of town, hard enough to get to,
far enough to be worthy for a rite.
The path ducks through tilted concrete piers
and the huge rusted bones of mining machines.

Two dug holes a hundred yards across and deep,
exhausted of iron and long left to boys, between them
only a bridge of land at its widest the width
of outstretched ten year old hands.

Wet is a giant's version of that Mayan sacrifice well,
quarried red walls leading the eye down
to water cold and paintrock red and calm,
without a ledge to crawl out on.
Where a kid was supposed to have drowned.

And Dry, a mountain cirque closed off,
cliffed and gullied, steep fans of taconite scree,
bits of moss green scattered down the sides
where groundwater seeps, and on the floor
the thread of a stream, a clump of alder scrub.
As deep, but a somehow more attractive fall.

So the boy comes to the ritual bridge,
as all the Southside boys do in their time,
to try the narrow rock and gravel path.
Small rockslides down the widening sides,
and all muscles taut across and back.

He walks barefoot and he walks alone,
without touching fingers to the ground.
A few bad places where he wants hands and knees,
where a loose pebble or a sudden wish
can make him choose between Wet and Dry.

He knows nothing of why. The ancient choice
is dared, and he learns the passage of Wet and Dry,
learns more than the fear his flesh sings.
Somewhere on that sliding edge he finds
the wish to be undone, that wish as soon erased
as he gains the trees and waiting hands.

The boy does not know he will walk that narrow path
for years. Each time he does not belong
he will hear the falling rocks behind his feet,
and inch across the night between two ways to die.

4

Finding the Snake

The second night Dinty Moore Stew
bubbled in the can on a rock while
something leaped in and out of firelight,
a mouse with grasshopper legs — then
flicked once, twice over the coals
and jittered into dark. Riddles
in night eyes. Everything gets caught.

After we pitched the tent we sculpted
beach, became godkings who
carved new kingdoms out of sand.
Argued rules for conquest and naming.

The first night strangeness scraped
the tentskin. What giggled
in the pines fled from what crashed
while we tried to imagine sunrise,
sleeping bags unzipped.

The second day we skinnydipped, a first,
snapped Brownie Hawkeye photos. I have one:
thin Jerry in water to his knees, a trimmed
birch sapling held upright between his legs.
Taut muscles of boys. Patchy first hair.

One day we wrestled and neither would give.
It hurt. The fourth day we explored the lake's
pathless circle. We swore loud and laughed,
climbed trunks and sucked sneakers out of mud.

I caught a big garter snake, all quick silent
straining. Jerry carried it the rest of the way,
head thrusting again and again out of his hands
never not trying to escape. I told him to let it go.
Shouts, and Jerry walked ahead, jaw a knot.

He carried the snake to camp and
threw it on the sand, raised the sapling
over his head and smashed it
down on the stunned spine. And again.

Together we watched the snake writhe from
the head halfway back. It kept yawning
and biting its dead part. I slid the sapling under
and carried it outstretched to the dock's end,
slung it into clear water. Kept silence.

Later I looked. The snake was out there
in five feet of water, alive, chained
to the sand by his broken half, upper half
silently weaving the water. Something old.

The lake became impossible. Couldn't swim,
strained water from the creek.
We did not speak, but separately
battered into waste the lands we'd carved.
When it came time to eat or sleep we shouted
blind. Slept rigid. Didn't touch.

Saturday we sat on our packs miles apart.
When the Ford rocked down the gravel to get us,
couldn't talk. My mother asked why.
We just loaded up and rode, one in front, one back.

Things refuse to die. Silence is the most
implacable. Every time I had to look it was still
weaving still aching for air refusing to drown.
I stopped walking out there to see. Knowing
is all backward. We get caught.

A man is right, a man
has to be right.
Is right the first time.
Is what right *is*.

A man doesn't do unless
he does perfectly.
Doesn't make mistakes.
A man imperfect is no man.

A man needs no help.
Shows nothing.
Holds his liquor.
Holds his heart.

A man is hard bone,
perfect warrior, strikes
in love. Must be alone.
Is safe alone.
Is safe alone.

The face flickers on and off as he reads,
sitting up against the pillows.
When he and a character fuse in
terror or delight or a moment of
great striving, and the heart
leaps out of words to overwhelm him,
this is the heat-of-tears-starting.
He can stay enclosed in this heat for days.

When Black Beauty is whipped, when
they cut the ears off Beautiful Joe,
when Buck breaks the sled from the ice,
the face melts and the boy doesn't
need to hate this surrender. But soft
bewilders. It is easier when Dave Dawson
joins the R.A.F. and strafes Nazis.

As she emerges curve by curve from our fingertips and palms, she becomes the mystery we must complete. Her breasts are handpatted cones, made after the torso and plunked on top. Cousin Bob and I create from empty beach the woman we have begun to dream. She lies on her back. Our hands shape better than we know, her lines as strong in the sun as in vision, and she is ours. Where her thighs meet we leave for last, for we don't know what to do. We simply poke a hole.

We know our parents, up the path to the cabin, will misunderstand. This sculpting is both art and necessity. But we could be hauled away by our ears.

So we make a plan for camouflage. We pat up a whole slew of extra breasts, lined up off her right shoulder in a row, near the water where the sand will stay damp. Next to the breasts, we stick upright in the sand a row of white pine needle clusters. Stockpile sand in long mounds along her arms and legs.

It works like this: if we hear a voice, Bob will push the sandpiles in to obscure her body lines. I will quickly plop all the extra breasts on her chest and belly, stick the pine clusters here and there among the new huts, and Presto! A South Sea Island village. The parent will ask, *What is it?*

The natives, we will say, *Worship this large fallen head north of the village. Here,* we will say, *Is a long narrow lagoon for their war canoes. And see here, at the end, the secret cave entrance, so the natives can avoid the climb up this steep hill to get to their huts.*

We don't have to use it. Little Cousin Petey, mad because we won't let him help or even stick around and look, stamps her back into beach while the sculptors eat lunch at the cabin. He knows we can't tell.

They must be close.
This is the man's imperative,
The boy's.
Neither of them know this to be true.
They would both recoil and bark
A laugh if it were said.

They hate each other.
The man does not put this in words.
The boy hums with it at night.
Both know this to be true.
It is not, it is a lie.

To caress the boy is to caress himself.
To caress the man is to caress himself.
Self cannot deserve it.
Impossible. But

They must be close, be
Intimate.
To touch is imperative.
To caress, impossible.
To hit is not.
They strike each other furiously.
Touch is touch.
They are close.

Some black odd-shaped thing he can't resolve, something with hair: he slides down to it but the air yawns like a vast mouth and he wants to leap backwards up onto the tracks. Crabs closer: the front half of a dog, tight curled fur. The dog ends just behind the ribcage, chopped off straight. It is dried, the fur cindered and dusty, the nose varnished. Lips snarl back from the teeth, the mouth opens to the dried black apricot of tongue.

He's seen his share of gutted deer, smelled the hot copper. It isn't the death, but the halving, the mummy hollow as a broken drum. No smell. Whatever rose from him is done.

He picks up a stick to prod it, throws it down. Climbs to the tracks, scrambles down the other side and finds the hindquarters, legs fixed in a trot, the loins collapsed in front of the hips. Town seems a long ways off.

He climbs back to the tracks, leery. Tries to see his body sliced, can't. Imagines the dog's headhalf falling down the bank, legs scrabbling, mouth open in surprise, the track trembling in the passage of the freight till all that's left is a dying rumble. When he meets his friends at the beach, he says nothing.

But that summer over and over he pokes along these tracks to the beach, watching air wobble above the rails, suit jammed under belt, towel shoulder flung, never sure he's going to look. When he slides down cinders and comes to rest dusting the headhalf, something slides down with him that he can't name. The mummy never changes.

There are three ways to the beach: the streets little kids use, the south tracks with the mummy, and the trestle way. He starts in August to walk the tracks to the trestle that cuts the north end of the lake. On the trestle way, the railroad bed falls suddenly away and he is twelve feet above black water dotted with pilings, stepping from tie to tie over gulps of light. It does something strange to the soles of his feet.

If a train comes, he tells himself, his feet will know it in plenty of time to outrun it, or to jump in and be all right, if he doesn't land on a drowned piling. He could hang by his hands from the beams while the locomotive tried to shudder him off. Likes that picture.

He takes the trestle way now for what's left of the summer. Never returns to the mummy. He doesn't think about why he is using the trestle way. He just knows it's time.

Art deco Indians and stylized feathers columned the walls at the Maco Theater, where we threw popcorn at Technicolor Westerns. The tympani swelled as reel Indians rode over the rise: **Pom** pom pom pom, **Pom** pom pom. Jeff Chandler was the Chiricahua chief *Cochise*. His daughter *Cincere*, fawnslim and pure — Jimmy Stewart the Indian Scout and I the Boy Scout both fell in love with her. After the movie I walked a mile home at twenty below zero and welcomed the pain. Unzipped my coat. I would be *Cincere's* ideal brave. Shucked my mitts. I would deserve her. Pocketed my hat. I showed no expression, so she could see my devotion.

It troubled me that she had to die. I didn't know the Hays Office Code insisted. A white man fell in love with her. She had to die. Better dead than red. The white scout who bedded a redskin had to be shot or knifed himself, but never fatally — just a coded reminder: don't mess with the natives.

Meanwhile the Chippewa reeled through tourist powwows on the Fourth of July. I didn't know yet that local high school boys drove up to Nett Lake with whiskey to buy a girl for a night from her father. The Chippewa were in front of our eyes, but I never made the splice. Real Indians were reel in the dark, *back then*, on history's spool when the lights came up. What we saw in the daylight we didn't see.

When the gondola crosses the screen
with the courtesan poised in the bow
and the boy first hears Offenbach's
Barcarolle, tears leap into him
where he sits in the darkened Granada
Theatre with a friend, and remain.
He has never heard so much.
After the movie they are expelled
into the downtown lights, where
he has a hard time concealing,
but so does Willy.
They do not look at each other or
anyone until they walk in
the dark between streetlights.
In the reflections of snowbanks
they begin to hum, still
not looking at the other's face.
But by the time they reach Sixth Street
they are glancing at each other's eyes
as they wordlessly sing the *Barcarolle*
over and over, and they sing it
under the streetlight, kicking holes
into a packed snowbank until their ears
crack with the cold, and they sing it
as they turn toward their houses
on opposite ends of Seventh, and hear
each other singing it for a block,
ringing it off the long arch of elms.
When they meet in the hall
the next day at school, they are shy.

The grass is rich and thick and cut close as golf green, with no purchase for the fingers. I lie on my stomach, as always, and see above me on the hillcrest the white-suited people being friendly around a lawn umbrella and white wrought-iron furniture. What I slide toward, what my fingertips cramp to avoid, is the cliff edge where the grass abruptly gives way to air, where I will fall hundreds of feet to sharptoothed rocks I cannot see but know are there. Out from the rocks is ocean shore, surf soundlessly foaming the beach in ragged rows. Between the rocks and surf is a wide sand beach spotted with the colordots of bathers and towels. In the distant center is a lifeguard's tower, also white.

My whole body presses the grass for traction, my fingers cling but gravity slowly edges me down the steep slope. I plead for help, as always, but the leisurely folks on the hilltop act as though I have no voice. Terror increases with each sliding inch. I will fall and fall twisting in fear until my eyes snap open just before the rocks.

When they said Grandpa Tromblee died in his sleep I thought, *What if he was dreaming?* Kids know if you die in a dream you will really die. And so far I have always wakened before I hit the rocks.

This time when I begin my fall to the rocks I am startled to hear my own voice say, *You are only dreaming, you will not die.* I stop twisting and let my body fall and fall limp to the rocks, and as my dream body dies I feel a painless wrench in my eyes. I am looking at my broken body from high in the air, blood on the rocks, oblivious sunbathers a hundred feet away, the white surf. I wake for the first time not in terror, sheets wet but my body already calmed.

I lie here amazed, thinking of the time I learned to use a beating's pain for strength. To have a voice in the night! I shudder with the power of letting go.

At the north end of the junior high hall,
ten foot Venus poses with heroic breasts,
her half-draped rump always dusky
with the leaping handpats of eighth grade boys.

On the wall down the corridor, paintings of
Sir Galahad pose stiffly under glass and resist
the temptation of Venus. Beneath each an
illuminated quote from Tennyson:

> The Knights of the Round Table,
> led by Sir Galahad, determine to seek
> the Grail, and gather in the Minster
> for a blessing ere they go —

Tom Boril dodges suddenly
out of the girls' bathroom past the painting named
The Castle of the Maidens, clutching
Rosie Simka's brassiere to his chest, its owner
bouncing furiously along behind him, past

> Galahad cometh to the castle seeking
> to deliver from their thralldom
> the Maidens who are the Virtues —

and collides full face with the Assistant Principal,
a mailed fist of a woman, her black helm
cleaving all claims and explanations. Hanging

from the fist by one ear, feet skipping
when they touch down, Tom
disappears down the south hall
below the plaster gaze of figleafed Apollo.

Every Sunday now after mass, he chants in the choir room as he disrobes,

O Lord, I am drunk
in remembrance of thee,
drunk on thy blood
which was shed for me . . .

As he prepares the wafers and wine, Father Boulet will never accept the boy's count of the house. He knows that if he makes too little wine into blood, he will have to consecrate it over again, and the congregation will grow restless on their kneelers. Mixing for twice the boy's count, he lifts and presents silver ewers, chanting.

He never more than sips, himself, so after all have shuffled to the rail and knelt while the priest tilted the cup and just kissed their lips with the Blood, he is left with a nearly full chalice of transubstantiated wine which must be drunk, and only the acolyte kneeling near the altar has not received the gift. When the wine meets the boy's lips the priest firmly tilts the chalice up and up, staying just behind the boy's gulping swallows. The boy's Adam's apple bobs until the chalice is dry. He has no idea that the priest fears God's Blood—but doesn't mind making this lamb of his flock wobbly-legged with holiness instead. So the boy chants in the choir room,

O Lord, I am drunk
in remembrance of thee,
drunk on thy blood
which was shed . . .

As he leaves the church after the handshaking, he trips on the first step and careens into two matrons, who use him all week as grist for their talk of the youth of today.

5

Gyrfalcon

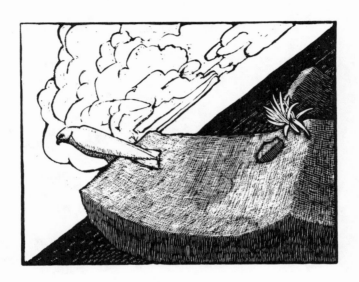

1

White bird on white
snow with a red fur small in one
lifted feathered-to-the-talons foot,
a hooked beak of black.

I watch its eye: a deep returning.
But this black gleam, catching mine,
finds me simply here, now. Nothing
more. It gathers in and leaps.

When it cries I know my own
voice although I have never
heard myself. I leap at
what I carry inside, how simple
and fierce and welcome it is, the cry

welling up out of me in union
with this white austere
mystery beating now
in my ears and eyes and beating
in my mind a white
flame against the dark.

Here is every graced cold thing:
snow, pine green, shadowed
feathertrack, talon black,
sweptback wing, blue distant sky.

He tries to find the white bird in words,
makes something like a creed:

> *White and clean and does not care.*
> *Black and fierce and does not need.*
> *Not caring keeps it pure.*
> *Not needing keeps it free.*

He says it before the nightly order of dinner,
says it during a beating, he says it
in the morning dark, delivering newspapers.

No one else has seen it. He doesn't know how
it could have a name, it is vision not
words. But he begins to doubt as he learned
to doubt that he could fly, the time
he pedaled calmly off the roof
without a bike because he'd dreamed it so.

Months later he finds it at the library, in
a color plate of raptors: **Gyrfalcon**, king
of falcons, that like ermine, only
ancient kings could carry on their arms.
According to the book, not found here.

He knows more. Gyrfalcon is in him,
too much to contain, yet he knows now
he has found what he must hold, or try,
that this white and beaked uncaring
is both *what* and *for*.

He would contrive them at first of mud and rocks,
or scrape them into sand, and people them with
the woodlouse and the ant, puddle and pond them
of whirligigs and water nymphs and fairy shrimp.
All the rules in his small worlds were his to find,
all that was allowed and not of leaf and heart.

There were small worlds dreamed and small worlds made,
and small worlds real but only capsuled in jars and tanks until
somewhere someday found, and there were roles to rehearse
to be the god of these worlds, rules to be learned
by all living there, all that was allowed of green
and biting and death, and worship was never a question.

As he gained strength, the whirligig gave way to the guppy,
the woodlouse and ant to the treefrog and snake,
and still all that was allowed was his, dying was his and birth,
but he learned the dilemma of gods. For his creatures grew
worthy and bright, the worlds would not stay discrete,
the borders broke down. The rules were no longer his.

What climbed in was the outside where all was allowed,
and the inside lost control. For god began to know worlds
unshaped to his dreams, and grew distant from
his own small worlds where the outside leaked in,
and sometimes forgot to water and feed—but he kept
the power of endings. The small worlds turned brown
and their creatures starved, while god finally learned
that the rules had never been his, except for the power
of endings. And the inside lost control.

Without the fist
there is no man

Without the upraised hand

Without the clench
the knuckles white

The man inside the fist
held tight

But the boy's flat stare
leaps the man's blood
from fist into face

and prints on the boy's cheek
a white negative of hand

The rocked boy stands
He will not see the man

The drift was probably driven fifty years before, the popple and jackpine on the pit floor were pretty good size. Willy and I were down in an abandoned test pit up past Higgins Location, on the Old Tower Road. At one end, deep in the rock, the old miners had driven a drift down and in for some ways—how far we couldn't tell, it was half collapsed. The timber shoring had mostly vanished into time. This drift didn't look too steep, mostly horizontal. It was beginning spring, one of those first excursions on bikes after the snow melts. But there was still snow and ice in the sunless inside of the drift, which made it spooky, so of course we went in, Willy first as usual.

When you crawl into something dangerous and absolutely forbidden, in a place where they could never find you, only eventually find your bikes hidden in the brush up next to a road nobody uses much except for a few gravel trucks, and you're boys but not completely stupid, after awhile you start looking around for reasons to crawl back out. Without saying that.

So as we were sliding down and in, knocking bones against slabs of rock, and down below could see the tunnel steepen into darkness, I looked up and saw a reason. Bats. Hibernating bats, hanging upside down and black just above our heads. We'd never thought about where they went in winter. There were thirty or so, lovely little wrapped packages of fur and brown leather. We all look better with our eyes closed and mouths shut and clearly helpless. Even Dracula, asleep, his lipstick in a prim almost-smile, waiting for night or the stake.

Hibernation. Such a mystery to be going on while we froze and shoveled and grew chapped rings of dirt on our ankles at the height of rubber overshoes. To be oblivious to shouts and snow and the absence of mosquitoes—to know the slow unbothered blood.

But what to carry them in? We knew at once we had to take them home. When touched with a finger they didn't stir, just swayed a little like black candle flames in a draft. How to carry them? Socks worked for garter snakes, the right size and shape, and long enough to knot. We only had a pair and a half without holes between us, so we gently detached the claws of three bats from rock and slid them headfirst into socks and tied them in. Tenners wet by now, and cold, we scrambled out.

The bats warmed up as we rattled gravel back to town, and the socks we'd stuck in our belts began to move. After we'd snuck them up to my bedroom and caged them in an old aquarium, they flopped miserably around. Little pushed-in wolf faces. And amazingly fast, in just a day or two, they died. Hibernation broken, warm and confused, without moving food. How could they not? I'd tried waving bits of liver at them, stuck on the end of a broomstraw, as best I could with the lights out, but I suppose the idea of eating without flying was too foreign. And later I learned about all the sounds they must have been making that I wasn't equipped to hear. I wish I could say I learned then not to cage things, but I didn't. I did learn something, though, about staying alive, where I was then. Hang in. Don't trust warmth. Stay cold.

The pint in the office drawer,
level dropping all day each
day, a nip, a slug, a steady
level in the blood, never enough to
lose control, the man's upper
lip kept on the verge of numb.

At night the boy plays bartender,
dishtowel around his waist,
knows how to toss a jigger
or two of whiskey
on the rocks, inhales as it
splashes over ice, hoists the tray
clinking into the living room,

knows that whiskey smell as
the woman bends over him in
bed, as it blasts from the cold
shouts of the man, knows it on
his own breath, how it keeps
him steady on the verge of numb.

Eyes, from that ceiling corner of his bedroom. From just beyond sight, over any shoulder. Whenever alone, the Watchers watch. Walking to school. From the bedroom window. Sometimes the boy forgets. A sudden start returns them. On the dawn paper route, from every shuttered window, curtains stirring. In the classroom. The Watchers. At the Newsette, sneaking looks at Argosy or Police Gazette. He never asks about it as he moves through time. Who would there be to ask? He assumes everyone has them.

So he becomes the Watcher of himself. Sees how he must look, how each move must look, learns the empty face, the falsely full. But he discovers a rule: If on his bed he reads and becomes other, he turns invisible. Even to the ceiling corner. But he fears the times his own eye flutters into sleep or any natural moment.

The Watchers are everywhere except—the second rule—the woods. There are other watchers there who scare the first away, the wild eyes he doesn't mind. Woods eyes can make fear, but they don't aim it. This fear is clean. In the woods he is visible even when he forgets himself.

But in town he must watch himself, so in the Watchers' watching he will not be discovered. He learns to wrap himself in semblance, as Claude Raines wraps himself in long white surgical bandage, around and around the skull leaving only the hollow eyes. This is the part before he goes mad.

The boy watches and wraps so well he stands behind his windings and all think they are seeing truly. His wrapping makes friends, works, drinks, lindys at the Legion, acts in school plays, laughs, even kisses. And in time even he thinks the gauze is himself.

But after years dancing becomes impossible. He no longer can tell when the watcher is Them or self. He no longer knows that is a question. But something is. He begins to see his wrapped seeming as the way he stays invisible—or is it a display of love for his wounds?

Pictures sift for his new knowing: *Ancient linen wrappings tattered and stained . . . fog . . . the Mummy's wrist and clutching hand slowly disappear into quicksand.* Wrong reel.

Shots flatten the night as he leaps through glass. As he dies, the girl weeping, his flesh slowly returns to the visible, first the time-lapse skeleton, then the overlays of viscera, veins, muscle, the moment of eyes . . . No.

Use this one: *Shots flatten the night, and shouts.* "Where'd he go?" Cut to: *Himself unwrapping bandages in a mad transport, spinning them off and dancing down the moonlit road, the long white ribbons dragged and dangled and finally snagged on bushes and left. He heads for the woods, a whirling in leaves.*

He saw nation in every cheekbone, every movement of a lip. Pops Schibel stood in front of Palace Clothing, greeting all in their mother tongues. Saw nation in a walk, the way a scarf or babushka was worn, and knew which of his seven tongues to greet. He apprenticed in Helsinki and Riga, Malmo and St. Petersburg, and in none of them could he own land.

Pops knew all these sons and daughters of hardrock miners who drilled underground in Budapest and Cornwall and Helsinki before they came across in the 1880s and 90s, jostling sons and daughters of the Canuck and Swede and Yank loggers who stayed to finish off the pine. Knew the steerage families from Italy and Montenegro, Finland and the Ukraine who came later with sharp elbows and notes on their clothes, knew the Greeks and Irish, the Baltic Jews, Chinese.

Nation was basic on the Mesabi. And where that tension ruled, so did clarity. A glaring clarity that let you know where you were at—like it or not. A restful clarity that saved the energy of *politesse*, saved work, allowed work. Clarity sired by Necessity out of Babel.

Here, even Italians said Eye-talian. To the rest, Dagos. Serb, Croatian, Slovanian—any Slav—lumped into Bohunk. Cornish were Cousin Jacks. Finns so lucid and sure they were simply *Suomilainens*, Finnlanders. Necessity: second and third-generation kids routinely insulted their friends to greet them, to defuse their parents' dislikes, their own suspicions. Insult with a smile. *Hey Dago, how ya doin'?* Insult to enable love.

Years later in Anthropology 1A, I hear a lecture about the Eskimo custom of *joking relationships*, crude ritual insults to lower winter tensions and prevent murder. Norwegian and German farmboys furrow their brows and push forward heavily in their chairs, trying to comprehend, and for a change, I lean back and cross my feet, happy to hear of other civilized groups in the north, knowing where I'm at.

SURPRISE!

See the pyramids along the Nile,
Watch the sunrise on a tropic isle . . .
Friday night dance, a kid
challenged for his girl—
when that fist loomed
and swelled and hit me precisely
on the bridge of my nose, I was given
the gift of perfect surprise:
I saw Stars. Everything black except
comic book Stars. POW!
Just remember, darling, all the while . . .
BLAM! Red Stars! White Stars!
A burst of immaculate discovery,
what I had always dismissed
became exactly true.
It was no comfort going down.

You belong to me. You belong . . .
Surprise is a test. Within
that first perfect moment, another,
surprise nested in surprise:
The song had it wrong.
She belonged to herself.
The rest was blood, black alley ice,
the circle of faces staring down.
She liked the fights.
And after decades I still absently
touch my nose, the crushed arch,
and don't quite know it.

The boy is looking for a tree.
His three pound axe is shoulder slung,
his legs are breaking trail through snow thigh deep.
Although he sweats, frost is crystal in his hair
and snowmelt trickles down between his scarf and neck.
His eyes are up and circling as he plows,
searching for a Christmas balsam to fill the green demand
his father placed, like perfection, in his eye.

The boy does not know, but stirring in his mind
is a picture held behind his eye for years,
from a picture book about a Christmas tree
who sought recognition, who to praise the Birth begged
to be severed from the root. In the story,
when the tree gets his wish and is cut,
God turns his needles into multicolored crystals
shining from inside. So much for roots.

It is well the boy knows little of his mind.
He is cold and stumbling wet and catching boots
on buried hazelbrush. He finds it hard to swallow.
Through fading light the snow hangs blue on boughs.
He believes he is searching for a Christmas tree.

SCHOOL MAIDEN

Edna Gay Schaaf, ancient
and dour, cracks one of her
canes across a desktop.
For choral reading, she has us declaim
World War One voices from the graves
of Flanders' fields, offering to blood
poppies but never forgetfulness.

Between choruses, between
the crack of canes, she continues
her ritual recital of the time
she shook hands with Teddy Roosevelt
during the Bullmoose campaign . . .

So purely impossible then
to imagine her fresh and parasoled
in a long white dress, a maiden's blush
across that ravaged face.
The ease of such vision now.
To the Colonel ever faithful, but
never forgetful of us, one of her canes
always whistling through the air.

THE LENGTH OF THESE GENERATIONS

My salty old grandma, polka dots and net,
French Canuck and four foot eight,
who stretched those tiny loins five times for heads,
loose-boned, the whisker-rubbing miner's wife,
walking old that day at the zoo,

with my mother at five foot two, a tailored peach
who married the mining engineer,
walking middle-aged now at the zoo,
with my sister in pink at five foot seven plus heels,
who pushed a stroller through that Easter zoo.

Grandma caught the titters and crowdflow
where the zebras were, saw the tumescent stallion
and cried out in her cackling old voice,
My God, girls! Isn't he hung!
The taller girls enclosed her quickly then,
skins burning like Easter eggs, and hustled her away

to me, astonished and stumbling, who could not stop
laughing, and picked up that tiny old bawd
so rooted in sense, in earth, and danced her in a circle
while we both cackled until tears which spoke,
together this once, of some lovely freedom in age,
and some loss in the length of these generations.

Beneath the concrete bleachers
of the Eveleth Hippodrome, lines of boys
in letter jackets routinely slouch both sides
of the corridors, wait for girls in their threes
and fours to come along, to
ricochet them with their hands
from boy to opposite boy, copping quick hard feels.
Some girls swear, some grow quiet and scared,
some like it, and a few in leather,
like Cookie or Tincups, dare them: *You wanna
wake up with your balls in your mouth?*

Above, the basketball tournament
semifinal game is suddenly stopped:
the PA crackles and announces simply *Joe—
Joseph Stalin has died. Stalin is dead.* The men
and women in the crowd surge upright and cheer
wild, throw deep sounds and shrill sounds
high into the Hippodrome while the kids
look around at them, unsure. The cold warriors
exchange smiling epithets with neighbors,
slap a few backs, sit back down.
The ref blows his whistle, tosses a kid the ball.

The boy twistfingers the flags on Gyp's legs,
iron-stained memories of chasing rabbits
through the ore dumps before he was hipshot and could run.

He was told it had to be, that Grandpa's last springer
must be put away, so after supper the man and boy
drive Gyp's nervous whine from Grandma's to the vet's,
without voice, the boy not sure why he was along—
to quiet the dog, he guessed.
It was not their habit to share.

Now and then one of them pats Gyp's head
saying *There, boy* or *Hey, old timer*
and it comes off awkward, like something badly rehearsed,
like the hint of lie in every Norman Rockwell illustration.

As they enter all of them recoil from the flaring
veterinary smell, from the air-hung pheromones
that burn terror into old Gyp's nose.
The man says simply *I can't stay here*
and walks into the night.

The boy lifts Gyp to the porcelain table
where dog claws skate forever into fear
while Doc fills a hypodermic from a bottle of emerald green.
The boy hugholds the dog, calms him, strokes him,
feeling on his palms the ulcers on that trembling neck,
wipes the mattered spaniel eyes.
Doc shaves the center of the left front paw
to expose the vein, squeezes it up, inserts the needle
and simply shoves, and before the needle is down an inch
the boy feels through the chest one brief jerk
and then cessation, and he is holding
nothing to his breathcaught ribs.

The old vet confides to the empty boy
that he keeps in his dresser next to his bed
a hypo of this crossboned green in case the crab
finds its way into his gut, and reminds the boy
that he can now lay down the limpness he is holding in his arms.
The boy thinks, through the dry center of a tear,
that beds are not clawmarked porcelain.

In this moment's emptiness the boy
loses all the space inside where Bambi lives
and Old Mother Westwind whirls away.
No room left for notions of a Gyp made young again,
chestblaze flashing, prancing up to some celestial hunter
with an eternal mallard in his mouth.
So he goes outside to see to the man, wondering
what will happen to the cooling meat that's left.

Outside the man stares into the dark.
He speaks no word of comfort to himself or to the boy
for fear of what will leap out from his voice,
that there would break from him his father's grief
for this last dog, his mind wandering
in the tubes and drains they'd broken Grandpa with.
Abandoned, he founders in his taconite gut.
The boy stands a few feet away,
and they share only the muteness of dogs.

6

Bracken Time

Sink below the surface of the bracken sea
to the narrow world beneath the flat
of fronds, sit within the curled duff
of crisp fern and old brownfuzz fiddleheads,
watch coins of white play through green
light as the breeze shifts fronds, or
slowly swim valleys on elbows
and belly and knees. Do this for all

unmeasured time. Then one year, duck
your head and scrunch and know you don't
fit any more below this edge of the green
brown world of hidden light where once you
made safety and dream, when searching eyes could
only catch the surface of the long bracken sea, for

now when you sit straight, the bracken is right
at your throat, now you pierce the edge,
are right through it, now you show, must find
a new way to hide, now you measure time, begin to

spill it, watch it fall through your hands like
the airy green water of the bracken sea.

The woman sprawls under
the dining room table, slip half
off and rucked up to her buttocks.
The outrage in the doorway looks
past her to the patch of carpet where
drunken buddy George snores
in his skivvies, past him to the living
room where the man and drunken pal
Sal sprawl half-dressed passed out.
As the boy freezes there the woman
lifts her head and questions his name.
He whirls to grab his jacket
and out the front door. *I'll be
early for school.*

Voices have been louder every night.
The stack of snapshots left in the hall
mail tray last week: a few of panties
draped across a sofa, nylons and bra, girdle,
skivvies, carefully placed. In others
the four posed in grinning pairs, toasting
each other, the men wearing the
women's underwear, the women the men's.

The man? *Nothing left anyway. Not caring
keeps it pure. I left my history homework
on the table.* The woman? *Nothing ever again.*
He knows they will never speak of this,
he will never. *Not caring keeps it pure.
Not needing keeps it free.* He cannot
imagine what there could be to say.
He cannot imagine not picturing them.
I'll be early for play practice.
He cannot imagine speaking again.

I am my own size. Naked I lie on coarse ground, under a bright sun. Hot and dry, stones under my back, but sensation is remote, without importance. I feel no need to turn or lift my head to look around me, just take in what is available to my eyes. Nothing I can see gives me a sense of scale. No trees, plants, no casual insects inspecting my skin. Just sun directly overhead, distantly burning, pale blue sky, brown earth of rocks and soil. No shadows stretching from boulders, no way to know boulders from pebbles. I am my own size, but of what proportions?

Darts of pain raise me onto elbows. I feel something inside me like a heaving for breath. I look at the rock my hand has curled around. Awareness swoops to that hand, the bone and blood moving from the inside. Skin and hair enlarged, detailed. A miniature black swan emerges from the tip of my thumb. It issues from a single pore and swells, its feathers sheen as if coated with a thin oil of light. The swan perches delicately on my thumbnail. Suddenly I am all fingertips and toes, and from the tips of each tiny birds grow — swallows, wrens, jays, mergansers, ospreys — all iridescent and shining. As they birth, they perch for a moment, spread their wings and fly. Soon hundreds of tiny birds circle above me. They begin to range over the barrens around me, and their droppings speckle the ground. Beyond my arm's length I can hardly see them, but still they give me perspective referenced to something beyond myself, although creation of my flesh.

There is a green on the ground now, and it is moving. Time shifts. The sun falls from overhead, whirls in the sky, becomes a ring of moving light. Seeds from droppings sprout and grow with enormous speed. Soon the brown is covered, the moving green covers the whole landscape except for treetrunk brown and the blue of sun-ringed sky. Growth flares my nostrils. Moisture is root-dragged from deep in earth and breathed into sky. Clouds form and showers fall, rivulets of white and blue in the tangled green. Time slows, the sun hangs still. I lower myself off my elbows, lie for a moment. I want to leap to my feet and drink these smells, showers, this waking into green. As I lift my arm, it passes through a cloud and shades a vast region of the forest below. I cannot rise without destroying it. I've found what I want.

The boy is in the green
urgency of light which spills
through terraced maple
leaves and falls to calm
the shadows moving on his face.
Sprawled on his back
in last year's leaves,
he is blinking, sap
has finally risen to
the corners of his eyes.

Bright shafts of green play
upon his body like sunlight falling
through clear water into
rippled sand. He
weeps, but cannot name
this easy welling
of the tears he will not use
for pain, until

he turns his head and
sees outside this light
which hollows him,
the tracery of veins the snails
have tongued from fallen leaves,
this blurred lace that nets
his shadows, and names
this welling *joy*.

Bellies of good times shoving
out of old Eisenhower jackets,
Nips and Kamikaze times,
Iwo and Tarawa . . . loud Marines,
the Legion Convention . . . *the girls!*
Bellies of good times:
This is my rifle and this is my gun.
Those goddam gooks!
Inchon was rough—
Not like the Big One, Bub.
Legion embroidered caps bob,
a sea of hands reaches for bartenders,
beer bottle rings, tapslosh over mugs,
starred & striped bunting fades over the bar.
Ten cent American flags hawked
at the street stand, hawked in the bar,
everyone bought, everyone proud.
American flags stuck in buttonholes,
tucked behind ruptured ducks and purple hearts,
waving in the hands of underaged boys,
flags playing swizzle stick. *Semper fidelis.*
Everyone bought. Bellies proud of good times.
On each flag-stick a thin paper strip
brush-stroked in red:

Nihon Tsukuri
Made in Japan

Gigantic Euclid trucks rumble up the ramp to the crusher, wait for the whistle, dump a forty ton load of ore. Down inside, Apocalypse, screens shaking, incredible din as chunks and slabs and pebbles and sands all sift their ways through screens, slamming on iron. After each load, chunks stick in the bars. New hires get to run out on the catwalk between trucks to unclog what they can. A six foot hook and a long way to lean to the weight of hematite. You hook and harry the chunks into the overflow if there is time.

You work with a clock in your head. The warning horn blares before another load will dump, plenty of time to run back to shelter. Then a second horn. The sometime game is to blow the horn when no load is coming down. The kids with the hooks will panic and bolt. Some miners never tire of this testing. With green kids, what goes around hardly ever comes around. Boys are fair game.

The man's hand is in
extreme closeup, lines
and pores, the black hairs
just above the knuckles
clear — the shock of its
warmth clasps the boy's
hard and quick, releases
as they both glance
away, turn to other
greetings in robes
and mortarboards, but
the boy is off-kiltered
at touching the man —
he cannot remember
touch from him except
in joined pain. The man's
hand fists in his pocket
now, the boy's hand still
glows, and he wants
to jam it under
a cold faucet somewhere.

He remembers none of it.
Blanked. But the body does
when a friend, a coach, any
male grips his arms hard,
the panic surges into cells, or pokes
him in the chest stiff-fingered, or
yells so the muscles lock and he's
afraid for his control.

He doesn't know this is
the meat remembering.
He only knows that in this now
his bones could snap
in his own muscles' striving.
Knows that in this now
die and kill blur into one.

He doesn't know he's blanked.
He struggles—not to fill it in,
but toward the child
never here, never heard.
Knows he needs a space for the child
to stand and grin like a fool
and not be touched.

The boy has no boundaries for
women, no skin.
Their pain winds through his nerves
like hair twisted on a finger
all morning.
All women are the mother
who is a wet wound
he can never close.
The women who need him,
the women he wants,
are the women whose grief
he exists to enter, whose wounds
he is to spill into
and somehow clot.
But he cannot, their pain
too snarled with his to separate.
He must not heal himself with them.

My first glimpse of our
three-cornered truth was
a visit to Grandma,
senile at the nursing home,
the last time, I think,
I saw her alive.

She was fifty years back
that day, in the company house
in Cooley Location, lost or
found in the past, and her girls
new wives. When she saw

me in my first beard
standing with my mother
at the foot of her bed, she
reared up on her elbows,
carnal smile on her parched lips:

So, daughter, so you've
brought a new boyfriend by.
I like his looks, is he French?
He's a handsome one — are you
giving up your husband now?

And that was where it was.

Looking back to Grandma
now, smiling with her demented
wisdom, I bow to her great
good sense of things as they are.

When he leaves, he will burn
across the world, skywriters
will name him in letters
a hundred feet tall, biologists
will speak of him in reverence,
his photo, pipe in hand, will gaze
at the reader from bookjackets.
Or by choice he'll labor in obscurity,
the reward the great work itself.
He will have a fine life. A fine life.

It's these people who gnarl
him now, this place. Leave.
All this dreary damned red,
and the man's slung hands,
the woman's hopeless craving,
the mirror's secret mad faces
will fog, wobble around the edges
and in a triumph of waking
dissolve from his brain into time.
His eyes burn with it: Leave.

But when the moment
arrives, all he can think of
is a waxed wooden floor,
bars of afternoon light falling
through venetian blinds
like a cello score, a velvet pillow
of green, a yellow windup tractor
whirring on its side, dustmotes
swirling in light above them
as if a throat had just cleared
or someone stood quickly
and walked from the room.

Black and white. So much more
like life than Technicolor. Print it.
It never fades, never
loses its edge. Beneath
yet another broken castle
the Wolfman finds
a huge body dressed in black
frozen into white ice.
The deep face is never—
Lon Chaney, Jr. scrubs the ice
with his sleeves—is
never clear,
wavers in torchlight
in the refraction of ice,
never clear but we
know that face, know
who it always is
before he builds the fires
to thaw the Creature
who is not dead and will not die.
Mind scrubs at the ice, commits
horror again.
The Creature never fades, never
loses his edge. And I
build the black & white fires
over and over, and
melt him into life.

7

The Color
of Mesabi Bones

THE COLOR OF MESABI BONES

In the Lone Jack mine in 1914
twenty three men with shovels and picks
curse and choke in dust and pray
in a motley of tongues
when the underground caves in.
They stay, the Lone Jack ore for a marking stone,
their bones stained red with leaching iron.

Iron birthed red, torn from the earth,
and miners and towns took its
colors and ways, reds of dust and rust,
of fresh blood and dried, of SCAB
slashed in paint across a store, of Indians
who would not disappear, of the Klan's fires,
Wobblies, union bombings, socialist Finns —
the only unred the blacklist.

Cars red with oredust halfway up,
and in November the gutted deer tied to fenders
streak the dust with blood.
Where it pools on runningboards, kids
dare each other to touch it.

Iron ore, iron oxides. Ocher, carmine, vermillion,
rust where the soft vein muddies the spring,
paintrock, stroked for centuries on cheekbones,
painted on the cliffs of Lac la Croix,
designs of another autumn, that vision lost.

Kids who live close to the open pits
mix paint from trackside dust
and for a game dip a finger
and mark their faces with their caste,
or smear the whole face, like Dad's.

The weathered basements of abandoned
company towns, houses taken off.
Hidden under tansy stalks in what
was yard, the red dust coats scattered stones
painted white once by a Finn miner's wife
to border the path now broken.

Working the underground drifts
in darkness and mud and carbide hiss,
in union suits, overalls, helmet and lamp,
rubber boots, pants and rubber coat,
and dripping from timbers through
five hundred feet of rock, water down the neck,
all stained the color of the Lone Jack bones.

Domestic reds: sinksuds, the bathtub ring,
the red rim of the drunken eye.
Red anything that stands to the wind—
house siding blown dirty pink, yet
the closer to the mines and tracks, the more
stubborn small white houses.
Red anything that runs or rolls on the ground—
no dogs are white. So much iron ore dust
you can't tell when a thing is rusting.

Coming off shift they all look alike,
Canucks and Bohunks, Dagos and Finns, all
the cold gritty red that won't wash off,
fingerwhorls, hands, fissured
necks like dendrites mapped in red,
and this is the color of the Lone Jack bones.

Pit descended, pit forgot, miners
crowd the counter of the Magic Bar,
red wide mouths barking slurs and laughs,
tired punchboards sagging like the thought
of the wife and kids in the VA house,
the lighted beersign waterfall
snared in cylinders of wet glass,
caught in drying rings below the faces.

The old men nodding, used to this,
watch the Wobblies pack the Range in the '16 strike,
riding the rails of empty ore trains,
watch them march, red flags and neckerchiefs,
watch boxcars of scabs unload
who can't talk English good either.

Hanging on the edge of the closed Majorca pit,
the abandoned washing plant, the windcraze of loose
galvanized iron trembles and bangs, hollering *time.*

In sadly named Aurora,
the strikers tear up boardwalks
for barricades, and Elizabeth Gurley Flynn
climbs up on top, daring the company goons to fire,
a homely Delacroix heroine dancing on tinder.
So many shot dead this year,
buried far above the Lone Jack bones.

The mine-dumps dwarf houses on the outskirts
of towns, foothills of gravel and rock dropped
first by glaciers, draglined and trucked
from the open pits. Above them brood
the worn granite breasts of the Giant's Range,
oldest earth, the blasting shaking even this.

The huge torch rallies of the Twenties
Klan, filling ballparks and picnic grounds,
the Jessie Lake encampment, couples sparking
in Model Ts on the hills above larking kids,
mom and dad, grandpa and gram in bedsheets,
burning righteous crosses across the Range,
native speakers all, or those who blended well,
shouting Catholics, kikes and anarchists!
Fire in the Lone Jack bones.

Iron ore. Hematite, from the Greek
haimatites, like blood, like what streamed
from the eyes of that old king, blood
of mother blindness, the vision lost.

Saturday night alleys behind the Legion dance,
the blood of smashed noses on white snow.
And every long winter's newspaper murder/suicide,
dried blood in a snowed-in cabin in the muskeg.

This dust, this red patina
on truck tires, shovels, coils of fuse,
draglines, timbers and railroad tracks,
this coating in throats and hawked handkerchiefs—

All night, locomotives full of steam
slowly huffing ton after ton of ore
up the steep tracks to the crushing plant, shuddering
and blowing off like horses at the top.

This drear overlay of rust
on tailings ponds and roadside weeds,
on sparrows taking dustbaths near the mine,
on the chain stretched across the company road—

And red is the color of bones.

INDEX

Abandonment	45
Acolyte	85
All He Can Think Of	120
Art Disguised	77
As Long as Your Feet are Under My Table	92
Beating, The	40
Black Swan Dream	111
Blanking Memory	117
Boy with Green Hair, The	46
Bracken Time	109
Breakfast Meeting	110
Broken Arrow	81
Canterville Ghost, The	38
Captain Tom	25
Changelings, The	31
Circus and Transformation	61
Color of Mesabi Bones, The	125
Conspirators, The	50
Creature, The	121
Dreaming to Power	83
Dumb Kids, The	32
Elements So Mixed, The	118
Empaths	55
Extensions	78
Faces of Ancestors, The	28
Falling of a God, The	63
Finding the Snake	73
Fluency	58
Forms Matter	21
Giant, The	15
Graduation Moment	116
Gyrfalcon, The	89
Hibernation	93
Home Movies	35
Infinite Regression	19

Invisible Boy, The   96
Keeping Steady   95
Kiss Me Goodnight   62
Learning Ketchup   48
Length of These Generations ,The   102
Love Triangle, A   119
Lozenge, A   13
Man's Creed, The   75
Marriage of Salamanders, The   67
Mine Town: *Being Screened*   115
Mine Town: *Blasting*   23
Mine Town: *Cultures Collide, A Quest Fails*   84
Mine Town: *Edges*   27
Mine Town: *Knowing Where You're At*   99
Mine Town: *Trick or Treat*   44
Mine Town: *Uncle Joe at the Ballgame*   103
Mine Town: *Victory in Japan Day, Eveleth, MN, 1955*   114
Mine Town: *What Are You Gonna Do?*   43
Mine Towns   17
Mummy, The   79
Outward and Visible Signs   68
Party to Enormity, A   104
Passage Rite   69
Permission   113
Quest in This Season, The   100
Reading   76
Red Maples   51
School Maiden   101
Scissor Man   56
Shaken Child   20
Sleep Tight   59
Snow Forts   41
Something for Everyone   14
St. Austell, Cornwall   16
Submariners   26
Surprise!   98
Tales of Hoffmann, The   82

Tentative, The   47
Terraria and Aquaria   91
To Sing the Fire to Sleep   34
Touching   49
Travel Collection, The   65
War Effort, The   24
Who Said?   42
World War II Premium from Battle Creek, A   22
Yellowjackets   37

Other Milkweed Editions Books of Poetry

Yehuda Amichai, *Amen*

Editors: Emilie Buchwald, Ruth Roston, *The Poet Dreaming In The Artist's House*

Editors: Emilie Buchwald, Ruth Roston, *This Sporting Life*

Ralph Burns, Roger Pfingston, *Windy Tuesday Nights*

John Caddy, *Eating the Sting*

Philip Dacey, *The Man With Red Suspenders*

Jack Driscoll, Bill Meissner, *Twin Sons of Different Mirrors*

Diane Glancy, *One Age In A Dream*

Phebe Hanson, *Sacred Hearts*

Margaret Hasse, *In A Sheep's Eye, Darling*

Olav H. Hauge, translation by Robert Bly, *Trusting Your Life To Water And Eternity*

Lewis Hyde, *This Error Is the Sign of Love*

Deborah Keenan, Jim Moore, *How We Missed Belgium*

Editors: Jim Moore, Cary Waterman, *Minnesota Writes: Poetry*

Joe Paddock, *Earth Tongues*

Len Roberts, *Sweet Ones*

John Caddy is also the author of *Eating the Sting* (Milkweed Editions, 1986). He is a third-generation native of the Mesabi Range in northeastern Minnesota, and the descendant of hardrock miners from Cornwall.

Caddy has received several fellowships, including the Bush Foundation Artist Fellowship, the Minnesota State Arts Board Fellowship, and the Loft-McKnight Award. He has also toured nationally as a winner of the Poets & Writers Writers Exchange Competition. Caddy presently teaches at Hamline University and for the COMPAS Writers in the Schools program.